THIS BOOK BELONGS TO:

_____

_____

HAND ME DOWN

♥

_____

For all the parents mindfully raising little feminists — especially the OG, Judi. -BST
For my favorite humans. JDTM - you rock my world. -KD

Written by Brook Sitgraves Turner. Photographs by Kati Douglas.
With consulting from Julia Moss.

ISBN: 979-8-9867049-2-0
LCCN: 2022918215

This book was printed in China in November 2022.

First edition
5 4 3 2 1

For questions regarding permissions, sales, or discounts,
email us at hello@littlefeminist.com.

THIS IS MY BODY
I GET TO CHOOSE

AN INTRODUCTION TO CONSENT

Written by **BROOK SITGRAVES TURNER**
Photos by **KATI DOUGLAS**

little feminist press

This is my body.

My body is mine.

I say "yes" or say "no"

with my voice and my signs.

Open arms for a hug

or offer a kiss.

I can fist bump, high five,

or keep space like this.

My grownups might help me

choose what is safe.

Like using a helmet

or washing my face.

I ask my friends

how they'd like to play.

When someone says "Stop!"

I stop right away.

My body is mine

and yours is all you.

Our bodies are ours

we get to choose.

A NOTE FOR GROWNUPS

Our littles rely on how we model consent. So let's practice asking for hugs and kisses, and encourage friends & family to do the same. Through your example, they will learn to ask before touching and to respect the response given.

But what if your little doesn't have a choice (e.g., bath, clothing, doctor's visit)? You can still offer options. For example, "It's time to put on your shoes. Do you want to wear your blue or red shoes?"

ABOUT LITTLE FEMINIST

LittleFeminist.com is a children's book club subscription and publishing house. Our team curates the best diverse books, creates accompanying discussion questions and activities, and delivers to families around the world. We publish books to fill the gaps we find in children's literature.